Nature's Children

HAMSTERS

by Dan Doyle

 Grolier Educational

FACTS IN BRIEF

Classification of the Hamster and the Gerbil

Class: *Mammalia* (mammals)
Order: *Rodentia* (rodents)
Sub-order: *Myomorpha* (mouselike rodents)
Family: *Cricetidae* (hamsters, gerbils and voles)

Hamsters:

Sub-family: Cricetinae (hamsters)
Genus and species: *Mesocricetus auratus*

Gerbils:

Sub-family: Gerbillinae (gerbils)
Genus and species: *Meriones unguiculatus*

World Distribution. Hamsters and gerbils as pets are found worldwide.

Habitat. As pets, in wire, mesh, or glass cages.

Distinctive physical characteristics. Both hamsters and gerbils are mouselike. Hamsters: most commonly golden; short tails, pouches for cheeks. Gerbils: large eyes and large, erect ears; soft brown or grayish fur, and long, furry tails.

Habits. Hamsters: Loners and nest builders. Forage for food at dusk and dawn. Gerbils: Hardy animals. Excellent burrowers.

Diet. Commercial pellets, nuts, seeds, roots. Fruits and vegetables when available.

Library of Congress Cataloging-in-Publication Data

Doyle, Dan, 1961-
     Hamsters / Dan Doyle.
                  p.   cm. — (Nature's children)
     Includes index.
     Summary: Describes the distinctive physical characteristics, natural habitat, diet, types, and domestic care required of these animals sometimes used as pets.
     ISBN 0-7172-9075-1 (hardbound)
     1. Hamsters as pets—Juvenile literature. 2. Gerbils as pets –Juvenile literature.   [1. Hamsters. 2. Gerbils. 3. Pets.]
I. Title II. Series.
SF459.H3D69 1997
636.9'356—dc21

97-5969
CIP
AC

This library reinforced edition was published in 1997 exclusively by:

 Grolier Educational

Sherman Turnpike, Danbury, Connecticut 06816

Set ISBN 0-7172-7661-9
Hamsters ISBN 0-7172-9075-1

Contents

Why are hamsters very popular pets? Owners love them for their small size, cleanliness, and soft, furry coats. They also like these creatures for their adorable habits, such as using their dexterous front paws to eat food.

There are twenty-four kinds of hamsters, but the golden hamster, also called the Syrian hamster, is the one most often kept as a pet. Golden hamsters have a beautiful, gold-colored coat. At maturity they are about six inches (15 centimeters) long. Like all hamsters, the golden hamster has a short, stubby tail and baggy cheeks, or pouches, for storing food.

The smallest member of the hamster family is the Dzungaruian, or Chinese dwarf hamster. It measures only two and one half inches (six centimeters) long. At the other extreme is the black-bellied hamster. This European "giant" grows to one foot (30 centimeters) in length—and has an appetite to match its size. In fact, one farmer complained of a black-bellied hamster that had a food store of nearly 500 pounds (230 kilograms)!

Holding its food in its front paws is one of any hamster's favorite things to do.

Greetings, Gerbil!

Hamsters are not the only furry little creatures that people enjoy having as pets. Gerbils are cherished pets, too, and for some of the same reasons as hamsters. Gerbils are affectionate, clean pets that are easy to keep. It's fun to watch them scurry and hop about, busy with their tunnel-digging chores.

Like other domestic animals, today's pet gerbils are descended from creatures that once roamed freely in the wild. (In fact, wild gerbils are still found in the deserts of Asia, Africa, and India.) These modern descendants, though, far outdo their dull brown ancestors in color, coming in everything from argent (silvery white) to gold, white, and black.

Adult gerbils reach a length of about four inches (10 centimeters)—and are twice as long as that if you count their long, furry tails. At the base of these tails are powerful hind legs that can be used for standing upright—or for making marvelous leaps!

A gerbil's strong hind legs are perfect for standing upright or making amazing jumps.

The Rodent Family

The rodent family tree has over two thousand branches. Along with hamsters and gerbils, it includes squirrels, chipmunks, guinea pigs, rats, mice, and even beavers.

Any rodent's most distinctive feature, of course, is its incisors, or front teeth. These large, strong teeth are extremely useful, especially given a rodent's diet of hard-to-eat bark, nuts, and bones.

Rodents do have one problem with their teeth; they never stop growing. If nature didn't interfere, rodents' teeth would grow so long that the poor animals would not be able to eat at all! Luckily, rodents' teeth are constantly being worn away by the hard objects that they eat.

Despite their reputation for being "dirty," rodents are remarkably clean animals. Both hamsters and gerbils spend a good part of each day grooming themselves and their young. They are even careful to create special "toilet" areas in their cages.

Like all rodents, gerbils have strong teeth—
that never stop growing!

Desert Dwellers

In the wild both hamsters and gerbils are burrowers, digging tunnels in the sandy soil and lining these tunnels with soft material. Avoiding the scorching desert heat, the creatures remain in their cool burrows during the day. Once the sun goes down, though, they hurry to the surface and forage for food. Like other desert dwellers, hamsters and gerbils get most of the water they need directly from their food.

Because of their small size, wild hamsters and gerbils have many natural enemies, especially snakes and birds. Over thousands of years rodents have developed an excellent sense of hearing and a very good sense of smell. These senses are their main means of protection from enemies. This is especially important since neither creature has very good eyesight.

Wild hamsters and gerbils must be alert at all times to keep themselves safe from enemies.

Latecomers

Dogs and cats have been domesticated for thousands of years, but hamsters did not become pets until as late as 1930. Gerbils gained popularity even later, in 1954.

In 1930 Professor I. Aharoni collected twelve young hamsters in the Syrian desert and brought them to his lab for research. His workers found the small creatures so adorable that they took many of the offspring home for pets. Today, nearly all pet golden hamsters are said to be descendants of the original twelve.

Gerbils have a similar history as pets. They were originally gathered in the Mongolian desert for research in Japanese laboratories as far back as 1935. In 1954 Dr. Victor Schwentker, a genetics researcher in New York, imported eleven pairs of gerbils from a Japanese lab. The animals' friendly, good-natured ways caught on with the lab workers. Today, all of the pet gerbils in the United States are supposed to be descendants of Dr. Schwentker's gerbils.

Hamsters are small enough to do astonishing tricks—or take an amazing ride.

*A well-equipped cage includes toys and other
things for fun.*

Getting a New Home Ready

When hamsters or gerbils are treated properly, they will provide hours of fun and enjoyment. But first their owners should make sure the animals will be comfortable and happy.

Before owners bring home their new pet hamster or gerbil, they should carefully prepare its home. Hamsters like their cages lined with wood chips and paper. (Newspaper should be avoided because the ink is poisonous for the animals.)

The best cages for gerbils are glass tanks filled with topsoil, peat moss, and straw. This allows people to watch as the gerbils burrow and make dens.

Cages should be placed in warm, safe areas that are free of drafts. Hamsters and gerbils can get sick if they are exposed to direct sun or to hot or cold drafts.

For the first few days in a new home hamsters and gerbils should not be handled. They need to get used to their surroundings before meeting their human family.

In the Lab

Some animals, including hamsters and gerbils, are bred for scientific research. Scientists studying genetics—the passing on of genes from parents to children—find hamsters and gerbils ideal because they reproduce very quickly. Hamsters have also been used to study rabies and leprosy.

Gerbils, for example, have helped us learn how unbalanced diets lead to heart disease. When they are given a diet rich in fatty foods, such as cheese, they suffer from more strokes and heart attacks than usual.

Scientists have guidelines for the humane treatment of lab animals. Yet lab animals do sometimes become sick and even die as a result of experiments done on them. Nobody likes that. But humankind and animals have benefited greatly from such research.

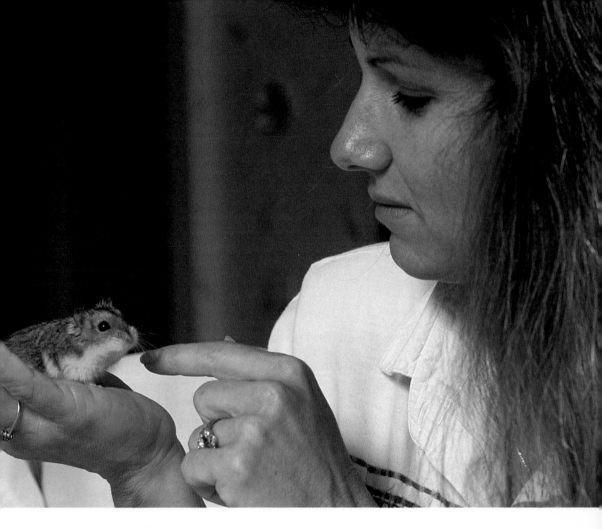

Both hamsters and gerbils respond well to people.

Made-for-Each-Other Gerbils

Wild gerbils live in colonies in the desert, so they are happier with other gerbils around. For this reason pet owners always should consider buying a pair.

It is a good idea to get two females from the same litter because they will get along best. (If a gerbil pair is made up of a male and a female, owners can expect babies—lots of them.) In addition, future owners should know that if a gerbil pair is not from the same litter, the animals should be introduced to each other before the age of eight weeks. This will help prevent conflicts.

Male gerbils are great dads and help their mates care for the newborn pups. They will share the same burrow, digging enough tunnels deep enough so that there is room for all. And once a gerbil chooses a mate, that is it. They mate for life and will not mate with any other gerbil, even if their original mate dies.

Hamster Loners

Unlike gerbils, hamsters rarely like each others' company. In fact, two adult hamsters put in the same cage might fight to the death. Wild hamsters live alone, as well. They have their own territory, which they mark with a scent.

The only time adult hamsters are together is during mating. Even then fights are likely to break out if the female is not ready or if the male is inexperienced. After mating, hamsters go their separate ways. Unlike gerbils, hamsters are not monogamous. The only other time hamsters share the same den is when a female is nursing her newborn pups. Once they are weaned, meaning they no longer rely on their mother's milk, the pups are pushed out of the nest. The youngsters then go on to find and make homes of their own.

Who's Who

Telling a male hamster from a female hamster, or a male gerbil from a female gerbil, can be difficult for the untrained eye. But there are a few external differences that make it easier.

Female hamsters and gerbils have rounded hind quarters. Males have longer, narrower rumps. On their undersides hamsters and gerbils have two openings. The opening closest to the tail is the anus. The one in front of that contains the sex organs. Female hamsters and gerbils have a shorter distance between the two openings than males. Male gerbils also have dark patches of fur around this area, with a noticeable pouch.

Hamsters are loners and rarely like to be in the company of other hamsters.

An occasional looking over will help keep
a pet hamster or gerbil in good health.

Choosing a Healthy Pet

The ideal age at which to buy a hamster or gerbil is when it is five or six weeks old. It should be alert and active, though hamsters rest during the day and could be a little sleepy depending on what time you visit.

A healthy hamster or gerbil should also have clean, sleek fur, and its ears should stand straight up. Gerbils should have long, straight tails without any kinks, bumps, or lumps.

Dull or runny eyes and a runny nose may mean that the animal has a cold or even pneumonia. Wet underparts, skin lumps, sores, scabs, or bald spots in its fur also indicate illness. Also, any hamster or gerbil that is either too fat or too thin may have a problem that is more serious than a lack of good nutrition.

Healthful Tips

A clean hamster is a happy hamster. The same is true of gerbils. Cages and tanks should be cleaned daily and scrubbed with disinfectant monthly. Gerbils are known to be nearly disease free, but they can quickly get sick in an unclean home.

Hamsters can catch infections from humans. Care should always be taken to protect them from disease and injury. Both hamsters and gerbils can be hurt if they are dropped, so pet owners must be very careful to handle their curious little pets properly.

Exercise also is an important part of a healthful life for hamsters and gerbils. Exercise wheels that go inside cages are a simple solution. Hamsters and gerbils can also be let loose outside their cages . . . as long as the area is safe from predators, such as cats, and dangerous objects.

Cleaning the cage is an important part of keeping a pet healthy.

Handle with Care

Warning! Hamsters and gerbils bite if they are not properly handled! That's true even if they are tame and friendly. Observing a few simple rules, though, can save owners from the sting of those big front teeth.

Hamsters and gerbils have poor eyesight, so they always should be given a chance to smell someone's hand before being picked up. This will calm and reassure the animals—and make them less likely to bite. New pets who do not yet know their owners can always be coaxed into friendship with a little food. In time, however, most gerbils will learn to recognize their owner's scent and respond in a friendly way.

The animal should always be scooped out of its cage with one hand and gently, but firmly, held around its middle. Hamsters and gerbils should never be picked up by their tails.

Sometimes hamsters and gerbils don't want to be picked up. When they don't, they will usually try to wriggle away. It's a good idea to leave them alone at these times.

Hamsters—like gerbils—should be gently held with two hands.

Clean and Sweet

Hamsters and gerbils spend a large part of each day washing themselves with their tongues and grooming their fur to a silky sheen. Indeed, they are very clean animals and are quite odor free.

Hamsters and gerbils have clean toilet habits as well. They will choose a space in their cage or tank that is as far from their nest as possible. Every time they relieve themselves, they will use only that space. Also, as both animals are adapted to the arid desert environment, neither drinks much water. This means that they urinate very little. Therefore, cleaning out the cages is not such an unpleasant chore.

Clean, fluffy bedding makes a gerbil happy.

Minding the Store

Hamster is an English word that is derived from an old German verb, hamstern, which means "to hoard or put away for use later on." And this, of course, is just what hamsters do.

Hamsters have baggy cheek pouches in which they collect and carry food. They use every bit of space in their pouches, filling them up like balloons. Back at the nest, they empty the pouches by using their forepaws to push everything out of their mouths.

Female hamsters sometimes even carry their young in their cheek pouches. People often think that the mother is eating her young, but it is just her way of moving them from one spot to another.

Hamsters' baggy cheek pouches can hold a lot of food!

Chow Time

Hamsters may be great gatherers of food, but like gerbils and most other rodents, they do not overeat. They will eat only about a tablespoon of food a day. Although they are not big drinkers, fresh water should always be on hand.

Hamsters and gerbils eat barley, bran, corn, rice, and wheat. They also like sunflower seeds, but seeds should never be a part of their regular diet. Sunflower seeds contain fatty oils, which are not very good for a hamster's health.

Both animals also love vegetables. An occasional fistful of carrots, clover, spinach, celery, or broccoli is very good for them. They love fruits, but citrus fruits like oranges or grapefruit should be avoided. Potatoes, iceberg lettuce, frozen vegetables, and anything that may have been sprayed with pesticides also should either be avoided or cleaned very carefully.

Like hamsters, gerbils love an occasional handful of broccoli or other vegetable.

Play Time

Hamsters and gerbils love to exercise and explore. Generally, their cages and tanks are too small and confined for them to run around as much as they would like. So it is a good idea for owners to set up areas where their pets can play freely.

These areas should be carefully checked for safety. There should be no way for larger pets or predators to enter. They also should be free of sharp objects, things that might be knocked over, or other sources of danger.

The areas also should be enclosed on four sides so that the hamster or gerbil cannot escape. Sometimes boards propped up by books can work well.

The animal will first want to explore and get used to a play area before it is ready to play in it. A lot of owners take pleasure in watching their pets get used to an area, using their busy noses to smell and their long whiskers to feel.

Wheels are always a favorite toy.

Escapees

Our little rodent friends are extremely fast. Hamsters can scurry away quicker than you can blink, and gerbils can jump even faster. But it is not likely that they can escape from their cages if their homes are well-built and made of plastic, glass, or steel. Sometimes, though, a latch isn't closed or a lid isn't fastened, and off goes the curious rodent.

Because hamsters and gerbils don't really know their names and won't answer when called, owners must use clever methods to snare any escapees. A foolproof trap consists of a plastic bucket of fresh greens and several books. Stack the books so that they make a stairway right up to the top of the bucket. The missing pet will soon appear and climb up, looking for the delicious food it smells. The creature will jump down into the bucket and have a nice meal, but it will not be able to climb back out.

Hamsters love to climb and jump, which can help them escape from owners who are not careful.

Mating

Hamsters and gerbils are very busy breeders. They can have as many as six litters in a year!

When it comes to selecting partners, hamsters and gerbils couldn't be less alike. Gerbils will mate only with their particular partner. A female hamster will accept any male suitor, but only if she is fertile at that very moment. Otherwise, a fight could develop. Breeders introduce male and female hamsters very slowly and wear gloves to separate them in case of a "quarrel."

Gerbils are ready to mate at ten to twelve weeks of age and remain fertile until they are nearly two years old. Hamsters are ready at four weeks, but the earliest recommended mating age is eight weeks.

Both female hamsters and gerbils are most fertile in the summer months. This is nature's way of helping the litters survive. Nests are warmer and food is more plentiful in the summer.

*Gerbils choose one mate for life. Hamsters,
though, have many mates over a lifetime.*

Mamas and Papas

Few mammals have as short a gestation period, or pregnancy, as hamsters. (The gestation period is the time measured from the fertilization of the female's egg by the male to the date the female gives birth.) A hamster's gestation period lasts only 16 days.

A gerbil's pregnancy lasts longer, up to 24 or 25 days. During this time the male is present and helps tend to his pregnant mate. Hamster fathers, on the other hand, are not present. Hamsters prefer to be alone nearly all the time.

Because bearing young puts a strain on the female's body, a pet owner should take extra good care of a pregnant pet. Additional food, as well as small amounts of eggs, milk, and cheese, are a good idea.

Dwarf hamsters—and baby hamsters of all kinds—make especially appealing pets.

Meet the New Family

Hamsters and gerbils give birth to very large families called litters. A typical litter for gerbils is five pups; for hamsters, it is seven. (Each baby in the litter is called a pup.) A pet owner who is planning on breeding hamsters or gerbils should first consider what to do with all the offspring.

Pups are born blind, deaf, and without any fur. They are completely dependent on their mother. Each pup is born singly and is covered by a skinlike membrane. The mother eats this covering to help replace some of the nutrients she has lost during pregnancy.

Newborn pups should never be touched. Hamsters and gerbils are extremely protective of their offspring during this time. If the pups are disturbed, the adult animals may instinctively kill their young, fearing that a predator is about.

Growing Up Fast

Hamster and gerbils mature, or grow up, very quickly. At what seems to be a very young age to us, they are starting out on their own.

After birth hamster pups nurse for three weeks before they are weaned by their mothers. Gerbils nurse for about four weeks. After that both youngsters eat regular adult food. By the time they are three days old, they have fur, and by two weeks of age a hamster's eyes open. It takes another week before a gerbil's eyes open.

After six weeks hamster pups wander out of their nests. Young gerbils, however, often remain in the colonies in which they were born.

As they approach mating age—which comes upon hamsters and gerbils very quickly—they will start making their own nests. Gerbil couples will share this den for life. Female hamsters will also keep theirs for life, sharing it only with male suitors and their offspring.

Showing Off

Hamsters are not just raised as adored pets and laboratory animals. They are also raised and bred to compete in shows. Much like dogs, horses, and other animals, hamsters are entered into competitions sponsored by clubs around the world. Most of these clubs are in England, where hamster fanciers, or breeders, are especially competitive.

Hamsters are judged on a number of criteria mainly having to do with their markings and their appearance. The winner at any one show is awarded a certificate. If a hamster wins three certificates, it becomes a champion. Not only will a champion be loved by all, but the owner will benefit. A champion hamster is very valuable as breeding stock.

Affectionate and lovable, hamsters and gerbils make wonderful pets.

Summing It Up

Hamsters and gerbils are wonderful pets for the entire family. But like all pet animals, once they are in a human home, they are out of their natural environment. This doesn't mean pets do not like their cozy surroundings. They might even like these homes better than the great outdoors. But as pets, they become the owner's responsibility. They are no longer able to do very much for themselves, including finding their own food. A good owner will accept this responsibility and enjoy taking care of his or her pet.

If an owner can no longer care for a pet hamster or gerbil, a suitable home must be found. Releasing a pet outdoors, whether in a parking lot or the woods, will almost certainly result in the death of the animal. A pet hamster or gerbil will not know how to fend for itself and most likely will starve or be eaten by a predator. Such cruelty certainly is no way to repay an animal that has given someone so much love and loyalty.

Words to Know

Dexterous   Able-handed; nimble.

Fancier   A person who breeds animals for competition.

Fertilize   The act of a male supplying a female's eggs with sperm.

Forage   To search for food.

Genetics   The scientific study of genes and characteristics passed on to the offspring of an organism.

Gestation   The period during which a mammal fetus develops in its mother's womb.

Hoard   To stash away food for consumption later.

Litter   A group of newborn animals borne at one time by the same mother.

Mating   A male and female getting together to produce offspring.

Monogamous   The practice of having only one mate for life.

Nurse   To drink milk from a mother's body.

Predator   Any animal that feeds on other animals.

Pup   A young hamster or gerbil.

Rodent   A warm-blooded mammal with perpetually growing front teeth.

Weaned   When pups start eating solid food instead of their mother's milk.

INDEX

Cover Photo: SuperStock, Inc.
Photo Credits: Betts Anderson (Unicorn Stock Photos), page 25; Norvia Behling
(Behling & Johnson Photography), pages 4, 7, 8, 11, 13, 17, 22, 26, 29, 31, 33, 35, 36, 41, 45;
K. Bogon (The Wildlife Collection), page 20; SuperStock, Inc., pages 14, 39.